Imitating *Nature*

From Gecko Feet to Sticky **Tape**

Other books in this series include:

From Barbs on a Weed to Velcro
From Bat Sonar to Canes for the Blind
From Bug Legs to Walking Robots
From Insect Wings to Flying Robots
From Lizard Saliva to Diabetes Drugs
From Penguin Wings to Boat Flippers
From Pine Cones to Cool Clothes
From Spider Webs to Man-Made Silk

Imitating *Nature*

From Gecko Feet to Sticky Tape

Toney Allman

KIDHAVEN PRESS
An imprint of Thomson Gale, a part of The Thomson Corporation

THOMSON
GALE

Detroit • New York • San Francisco • San Diego • New Haven, Conn. • Waterville, Maine • London • Munich

THOMSON

GALE

For more information, contact
KidHaven Press
27500 Drake Rd.
Farmington Hills, MI 48331-3535
Or you can visit our Internet site at http://www.gale.com

LIBRARY OF CONGRESS CATALOGING-IN-PUBLICATION DATA

Allman, Toney.
  From gecko feet to sticky tape / by Toney Allman.
    p. cm. — (Imitating nature)
  Includes bibliographical references and index.
  ISBN 0-7377-3489-2 (hard cover : alk. paper)
   1. Adhesives—Juvenile literature. 2. Adhesive tape—Juvenile literature. 3. Geckos—Anatomy—Juvenile literature. 4. Inventions--Juvenile literature.   I. Title. II. Series.
  TP968.A62 2006
  668'.38—dc22   2005018680

Printed in The United States of America

Contents

CHAPTER 1

Gecko Sticking Power

More than 2,000 years ago, a famous Greek thinker named Aristotle noticed that some lizards, called geckos, could run straight up walls and walk upside down on ceilings. He wondered how the geckos did it. Geckos do not use their claws for clinging. Their feet do not have suction cups or glue. Geckos do not even have extra-strong legs or tails for climbing. Aristotle described the mystery of gecko sticking power, but he could not solve it. Today, scientists have finally found the answer to the puzzle. Understanding the gecko's remarkable ability is teaching these scientists to imitate gecko feet and invent tape that never loses its stick.

Geckos

Geckos live all around the world, and there are hundreds of **species**. They range in size from about a half inch (1.5cm) to about 14 inches (35.5cm) long. Of all the geckos, the tokay gecko is the most talented climber. It is one of the best climbers in the world.

A mourning gecko uses its sticky feet (close-up, inset) to walk straight up a glass wall.

Tokay geckos live in warm, tropical places in Southeast Asia. They are large geckos, measuring more than 13 inches (33cm) long. Their bodies are covered with reddish brown spots that help them blend in with the trees and cliffs where they live. The geckos run and climb everywhere, searching for insects to eat and escaping from enemies.

Gecko Feet

Tokay geckos can climb so well because of their special feet. Each gecko foot looks like a fat little hand, but the "fingers" are really toes. The undersides of the five toes are wide and flat. These toe pads are the secret of gecko climbing power. Under a microscope, the toe pads can be seen to be made up of soft scales. The scales have millions of microscopic hairs, called **setae**, which branch into even more hair tips, something like the

Like all geckos, this leopard gecko is an excellent climber.

split ends of a human hair. Each gecko foot has 500,000 hairs. At the tip of each hair are about 1,000 even tinier hairs. These are called **spatulae** because the ends look like tiny spatulas. Altogether, geckos have a billion spatulae that resemble heads of broccoli at the ends of the setae. These spatulae can stick to nearly anything.

Because of their setae and spatulae, geckos can run straight up a cliff at up to 3.3 feet (1m) per second. They can hang upside down by one toe, stretch out, and grab a bug meal. In captivity, a tokay gecko can scamper straight up a pane of glass or race across the ceiling.

Talented Little Toes

Many scientists at different universities worked together to figure out gecko sticking power. They call

The soft scales of a tokay gecko's toe pads (below) make it easy for the lizard to climb up a log (left).

Amazing Feet!

1 Geckos have special feet that help them stick to almost any surface.

2 Each toe is covered with small, soft scales.

3 The scales are made up of millions of microscopic hairs called setae. The tips of the setae are split into even tinier hairs. Amazingly, these tiny hairs are themselves split into supertiny hairs called spatulae.

4 Geckos have a billion spatulae that look like little heads of broccoli. Here, a gecko's broccoli-like spatulae are magnified 425 times with an electron microscope.

themselves the Gecko Team. One of these scientists, Robert Full, studied geckos in his Poly-PEDAL Laboratory at the University of California, Berkeley. In his laboratory, Full took pictures of running tokay geckos with high-speed cameras that recorded every bit of movement of every step of each gecko foot. When he studied his film, Full made an amazing discovery. Gecko toes work like the party favors that children blow at birthday celebrations. These toys curl up and then uncurl when they are blown. Gecko toes work the same way. The setae curl up to peel a toe off the surface and then uncurl to lie flat and press the spatulae into the surface. Each toe curls and uncurls 30 times a second when the gecko is running. With each step, the gecko sticks to its running surface, and then rolls up its toe to get

Grumpy Creatures

Tokay geckos are very unfriendly animals, and they can deliver painful bites to people who bother them. As well, they do not become tame in captivity. Scientists on the Gecko Team, such as Robert Full, always wear thick leather gloves when they have to handle geckos for their experiments.

Robert Full wears thick gloves to protect his hand from the painful bite of a tokay gecko.

More than Enough Strength

● If all a tokay gecko's setae on only two feet were touching a ceiling at the same time, they could hold a kid who weighs 125 pounds. If all the setae on four feet were touching, they could hold someone who weighs 250 pounds!

unstuck and keep running forward. A gecko unpeels its toes from a cliff just as a person peels a piece of adhesive tape off a wall.

But what is so special about setae and spatulae that makes them stick so well? The Gecko Team had to do many more experiments to find the answer to that question.

This view of the underside of a tokay gecko shows the lizard's powerful, sticky feet.

CHAPTER 2

In the Gecko Lab

Kellar Autumn is one of the leaders of the Gecko Team. At his laboratory at Lewis and Clark College in Oregon, he was determined to figure out how setae and spatulae get their stickiness. Then, other Gecko Team scientists could use his discovery to imitate gecko setae.

Spatulae and Molecules

In 2000 Autumn discovered that geckos stick because their spatulae are so tiny that they cling to the **molecules** in their running surfaces. Everything in the world is made up of microscopic building blocks called molecules. These molecules are held together by a weak magnetic-like force. The attraction is much weaker than a toy magnet's, but it is strong enough to keep things from coming apart. Trillions of molecules cling together in a sheet of glass, for example.

Spatulae are only 200 **nanometers** across. A nanometer is a billionth of a meter. The spatulae are so tiny that they actually mingle with the molecules in

Kellar Autumn (left) and his students study a tokay gecko to discover what makes the lizard's feet so sticky.

Gecko Sticking Power
Illustration of a microscopic gecko hair

Tiny hairs at
tip of seta

Spatulae

Seta

Scale

Under a powerful microscope, the bottom of a gecko's foot shows its thousands of small scales made up of a billion microscopic hairs. The smallest hairs, called spatulae, are where the gecko gets its sticking power. Spatulae can stick to almost anything.

the gecko's running surface. The spatulae cling to the running surface molecules almost like miniature magnets. Because millions of spatulae cling to the surface at the same time, the many weak attractions become a strong force that keeps the gecko sticking anywhere.

When the gecko changes the angle of the bendable spatulae by rolling up its toe, the attraction is broken and the foot lifts up easily.

No Baths Needed

Autumn also discovered why gecko feet never lose their stick. Any kind of man-

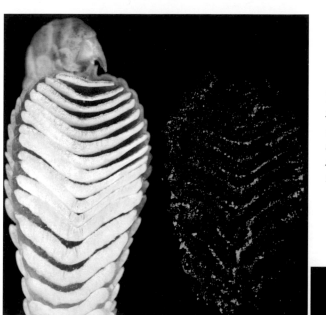

The tokay gecko's self-cleaning toes (far left) leave dirt behind (left), so its feet never lose their stick.

made tape loses its stick because dirt and wetness stick to the tape. Geckos never groom their feet, but their feet are always clean and sticky, even when geckos walk in dirt, dust, water, or sand. Autumn found out that water and dirt roll off gecko feet because not enough spatulae touch a speck of dirt or drop of water at the same time. Since the setae are not clinging to enough molecules to stick, the dirt and water roll away, and gecko feet clean themselves. If the Gecko Team could invent a self-cleaning tape that worked like gecko feet, such tape would stick even in mud or underwater.

Making Sticky Setae

At Berkeley, scientist Ron Fearing was excited to learn how gecko setae and spatulae work. He decided to build setae of his own. In 2002 he built two artificial setae. One was made of rubber, and the other was made of polyester. Under a microscope, he looked at how well the hairs clung to a surface. Each hair stuck to the surface, just as a gecko hair would. However, Fearing would have to make millions of setae before he had a piece of tape that would stick the way gecko feet can.

Making millions of setae was hard to do, but in 2003, Fearing succeeded. He made an array of polyester hairs that had spatulae and really stuck to things. The artificial hairs were nowhere near as sticky as gecko hairs, though. Fearing and his team measured the stickiness of the array under a microscope. They found that the artificial hairs clung only about one-twentieth as well as the real thing.

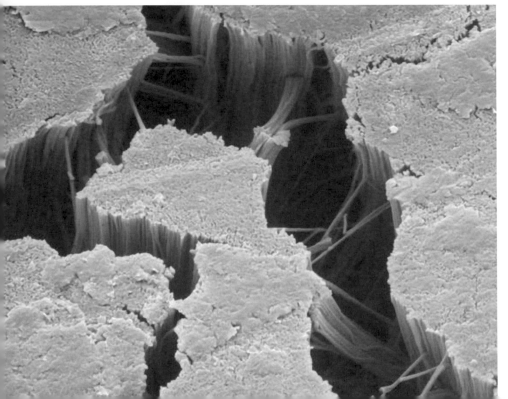

Ron Fearing's artificial hairs (magnified 2,500 times under a microscope) are sticky, but they do not cling as well as the hairs on a gecko's feet.

Amazing Setae

The Gecko Team discovered that just one seta has the clinging power to lift the weight of an ant. A million setae are so small that they would fit on a dime but could lift a child who weighs 45 pounds.

Still, Fearing's array brought the Gecko Team one step closer to inventing setae that were as sticky as gecko setae. As the team continued to research ways to improve their artificial hairs, another scientist learned about their work. Andre Geim, at the University of Manchester in England, thought he could help. He had built computer chips, so he was used to working with very tiny things. He decided to try to make a piece of gecko tape that would work just like a gecko toe.

CHAPTER 3

Gecko Tape

In 2003 Andre Geim made a piece of geckolike tape. Someday soon, people may be able to stick to ceilings, or equip robots with sticky feet, or wear the same ouchless bandage over and over. The Gecko Team can think of dozens of uses for gecko tape.

Setae for Spider-Man

Geim made his gecko tape using the same equipment that he uses to make computer chips. He built his tape under an **electron microscope**, so that he could make the setae extremely tiny. His finished tape was only about the size of a postage stamp, but it had millions of setae. It was 0.4 inch (1cm) square. The setae were attached to a flexible ribbon so that they could bend and press into a surface.

Geim took a Spider-Man action figure and hung it from a plate of glass on his office ceiling. Spider-Man stayed safely stuck for several hours. Then Geim easily

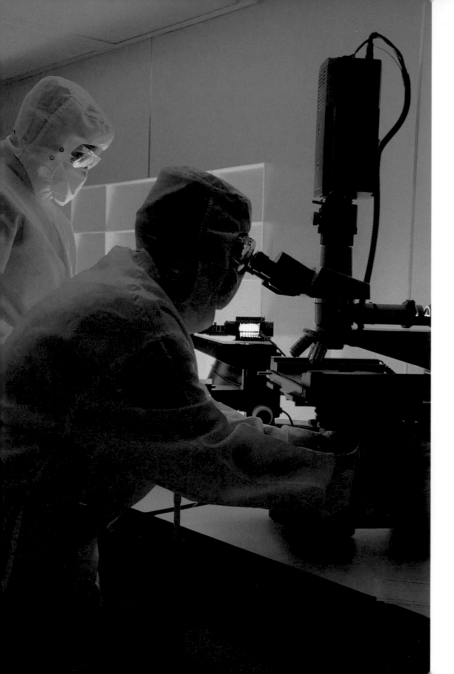

peeled it off. Geim thought about making a bigger piece of tape and hanging one of his students out the window. Many of his students wanted to try it, but Geim decided to stick with the Spider-Man toy.

Geim's gecko tape is sticky, but it has a problem. It can be used seven or eight times, but it gradually loses its sticking power because the setae clump together as they pick up water from the air. Geim is back in his lab, trying to find a material for his setae that repels water as well as gecko feet do.

Kellar Autumn and Ron Fearing have a different idea. They are trying to space the setae farther apart on their tape, so that the hairs cannot clump together. Robert Full believes that in less than five years, one of the scientific teams will have solved the problem and invented tape that works as well as real gecko setae.

Peel and Stick

Gecko setae have to bend at just the right angle to stick. This allows the setae to mingle with and cling to surface molecules. As soon as the angle changes, the attraction disappears, and the setae pop right off. A gecko rolls up its toes to change the angle. A person wearing a gecko glove would have to learn to peel his or her hand away from the ceiling, just as a gecko peels off its foot. With practice, a person could learn to walk in gecko shoes or travel hand-over-hand across a ceiling using a peeling motion.

A gecko curls the toes on its back foot at just the right angle and lifts it from a glass wall.

From Gecko Feet to Sticky Tape

Sticky Hands and Feet

When that time comes, people will have gecko gloves and gecko shoes. Gloves and shoes made with gecko tape would stick everywhere. Mountain climbers, for example, could use the gloves to cling to the tiniest projections, haul themselves straight up cliffs, and never risk deadly falls. Firefighters wearing gecko tape could climb up buildings and rescue people.

Robots could wear gecko tape on the bottoms of their feet, just as people would wear gecko shoes. Such robots could explore Mars, climb anywhere, and never risk falling or breaking. On Earth, small robots with gecko feet could walk underwater to explore sunken ships or make submarine repairs.

Two small robots inspired by geckos have already been

Gecko gloves may one day be used by mountain climbers to keep them safe from falls.

invented. They were built by the iRobot Company with Full's help. The robots are named Mecho-Gecko and Bull-Gecko. Mecho-Gecko has little sticky feet, and Bull-Gecko has treads like a bulldozer. Neither robot has real setae yet, but they wear a kind of tape that lets them climb and roll up their

The iRobot Company's Mecho-Gecko robot (left) uses its feet to cling to a glass wall while a real gecko does the same.

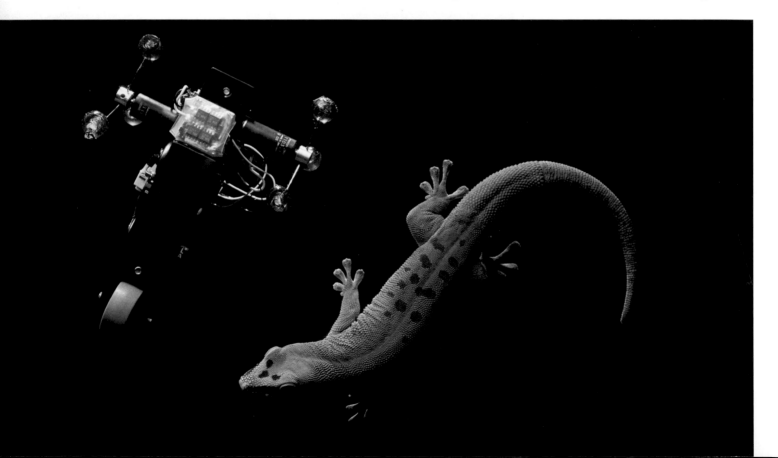

Gecko Gravity

Astronauts on the International Space Station cannot walk in the weightlessness of space. They float or swim through the air to get from place to place. If astronauts had gecko shoes, they could walk in space as normally as they do on Earth, even though there is no gravity. Gecko tape would hold them to the floor.

An astronaut (inset) repairs a section of the International Space Station. Gecko shoes and gloves could help make spacewalks safer for astronauts.

feet and treads the way geckos do. Someday, scientists hope to equip a robot with real setae that cling everywhere and never get dirty.

Gecko Tape Power

When hairy tape becomes a reality, it will make picture-hanging tape that does not leave marks on walls, duct tape that sticks to things that are dirty or wet, and automobile tires that cling to roads. Since setae will be so tiny and clean, doctors will even be able to use gecko tape in surgery. They will seal wounds and surgical incisions with gecko tape instead of stitches.

Robert Full believes that gecko tape will mean a revolution in the way people live. He says that in less than ten years, gecko tape will find its way into everyday life. Someday, everyone may be able to crawl up walls like Spider-Man, thanks to a tape inspired by sticky gecko feet.

Glossary

electron microscope: A kind of microscope that uses very tiny particles called electrons to look at objects that are too small to see with a regular light microscope.

molecules: The building blocks of all substances.

nanometers: Measurements of billionths of meters. "Nano" means one-billionth and is used to describe extremely tiny particles, sizes, and structures.

setae (SEE tee and SEE tah for "seta"): The microscopic hairs that cover gecko toes. "Setae" is plural, and "seta" is singular, for one hair.

spatulae (SPACH uh lee): The hundreds of spatula-shaped pads at the tips of the setae. "Spatula" is singular.

species: A basic category of animals that are closely related to one another and can breed with each other.

For Further Exploration

Books

Sonia Hernandez-Divers, *Geckos*. Chicago: Heinemann Library, 2003. Many people enjoy keeping geckos as pets. In this book, readers can learn not only about the lives of geckos, but also about how to feed and care for them. The gecko described in this book is a leopard gecko.

Gail B. Stewart, *Microscopes*. San Diego: KidHaven Press, 2003. Discover the different kinds of microscopes and how scientists use them. See some amazing magnified images, too.

Web Sites

Gecko Locomotion in Nature (www.lclark.edu/~autumn/T.scincus.html). See a gecko running in its natural environment.

Gecko Locomotion on a Treadmill (www.lclark.edu/~autumn/N.asper.html). Watch a gecko running on a treadmill in Kellar Autumn's lab.

Geckos (www.eas.sa.edu.au/kidswork/jay/indexb.html). This student project from Australia's East Adelaide School describes where geckos live, what they eat, why they are special, and much more.

How Geckos Stick to Walls (www.lclark.edu/
~autumn/private/u38j47a0t). This site features pho-
tographs of gecko feet and microscopic setae from
the Autumn Lab and the Poly-PEDAL Laboratory.

**Science News for Kids, How a Gecko Defies Grav-
ity.** (www.sciencenewsforkids.org/articles/20031119/
Feature1.asp). Read a feature story about Kellar Autumn and solving the mystery of gecko feet.

**Science News for Kids, Sticking Around with
Gecko Tape.** (www.sciencenewsforkids.org/articles/
20030611/Note2.asp). See a picture of the Spider-
Man toy that Andre Geim stuck to the ceiling with
gecko tape. Read the story of his invention.

Unlocking the Secrets of Animal Locomotion
(www.berkeley.edu/news/media/releases/2002/
09/rfull/robots.html). Discover some robots inspired by animals, and watch a movie of Mecho-
Gecko.

Index

Picture Credits

Cover: (From left) PhotoDisc; Getty Images; Dennis Kunkel/Visuals Unlimited; Courtesy of Andre Geim

© 2004 Kellar Autumn, Lewis & Clark College, Portland, Oregon, 13, 15, 17 (both), 22

© Bettmann/CORBIS, 9 (both)

Courtesy of R. Fearing/U.C. Berkeley, 18

Courtesy of Andre Geim, 26

Getty Images, 7, 10 (bottom left), 12, 21

Victor Habbick Visions, 10, 12, 16

© Dr. Dennis Kunkel/Visuals Unlimited, 10 (bottom right)

© Peter Menzel/www.menzelphoto.com, 11, 24

NASA, 25

PhotoDisc, 8

Photos.com, 23

About the Author

Toney Allman holds degrees from Ohio State University and the University of Hawaii. She currently lives in Virginia beside the Chesapeake Bay.